E. D Root

Sakya Buddha

a versified, annotated narrative of his life and teachings, with an excursus containing citations from the Dhammapada, or Buddhist canon

E. D Root

Sakya Buddha
a versified, annotated narrative of his life and teachings, with an excursus containing citations from the Dhammapada, or Buddhist canon

ISBN/EAN: 9783337246846

Printed in Europe, USA, Canada, Australia, Japan

Cover: Foto ©Lupo / pixelio.de

More available books at **www.hansebooks.com**

SAKYA BUDDHA:

A

Versified, Annotated Narrative

OF HIS

LIFE AND TEACHINGS;

WITH

AN EXCURSUS,

CONTAINING

Citations from the Dhammapada, or Buddhist Canon.

By E. D. ROOT,

AN AMERICAN BUDDHIST.

"The more I learn to know Buddha, the more I admire h'm, and the sooner all mankind shall have been made acquainted with his doctrines the better it will be, for he is certainly one of the heroes of humanity."—Dr. FAUSBOLL.

NEW YORK:
CHARLES P. SOMERBY,
18 Bond Street.
1880.

Copyrighted,
By C. P. Somerby,
1880.

C. P. Somerby,
Electrotyper and Printer,
18 Bond-st., N. Y.

PREFACE.

In presenting this unpretentious poem to the world, I am not certain that the cadence of its numbers will strike favorably the public-ear. Should it fail, through its dearth of afflatus, to arrest the attention of American scholars, I am prone to believe that in India, where the grand ethical teacher gifted his birth-land with fame's proud laurels, it will live in the hearts of many of his followers, and, peradventure, be enstamped with the sigil of immortality.

The volumes containing the Life and Teachings of Buddha, from which the material that girds the poem has been gleaned, are expensive, and beyond the reach of the mass of readers.

I have epitomized, and brought within the scope of the masses (to whom those volumes are inaccessible) all that is needed to form a correct biographical narrative of the keenest-minded of all religious, Heaven-sent Ariels.

I have endeavored with copious annotatations to render plain many incidents interwoven with the career of Buddha which could not have been easily wrought in rythmic numbers.

In launching my epical poem upon the bournless sea of literature, I offer no apology, and make no cringing appeal to the mercy of critical reviewers; and should my humble effort fail to meet their approval, or be rejected by them as unmeritorious, let their censuring frowns forever rest upon the ill-starred narrative of the all-adored Founder, who has borne betimes the struggling author over life's storm-vexed surges, when fate-girded Hope was whelmed 'neath affliction's dark waters.

Deep-roused by true missionary zeal to blazon far and wide the incomparable Law of the gentle Lord Buddha, and knowing beyond a shadow of uncertainty, accompanied by an overwhelming cogency of evidence, that my earth-flown friends, hovering near the fringe of supernal spheres, are swaying and shaping my anomalous career, I am lifted toweringly above the narrow judgment of the daintified, cynical reviewer, who will find it easier to demolish a fortress than to erect one that will be impregnable.

The reader will please accept my assurance with all confidence that the poem contains nothing dispraising the Christian religion, nor the sublime teachings of the Godman Nazarene.

Hoping that this candid avowal will disarm all unreasonable prejudice, and prepare the mind for a careful perusal of my truth-founded narrative, I remain, kind reader, yours in mortal bonds, striving to attain that glorious, spiritual life, which blooms beyond the grave with ineffable grandeur.

E. D. R.

FORESTVILLE, Conn.,
October, 1879.

PRELIMINARY OBSERVATIONS.

It was the gifted poet Goethe who gave to the world the following paradoxical apothegm: "He who knows only one language knows none." To this the lettered Max Müller adds: "He who knows only one religion knows none. As a true knowledge of a language requires a knowledge of languages, thus a true knowledge of a religion requires a knowledge of religions; and however bold the assertion may sound, that all languages have an Oriental origin, true it is that all religions, like the suns, have risen from the East."

In the elucidation of this paradox, the

distinguished philologist relevantly queries: "Could Goethe have meant that Homer did not know Greek, or that Shakspeare did not know English, because neither of them knew more than his own mother-tongue? No! What was meant was that neither Homer nor Shakspeare knew what that language really was which he handled with so much power and cunning. . . . It becomes clear at once that the most gifted poet and most eloquent speaker, with all their command of words and skillful mastery of expression, would have but little to say if asked what language really is! The same applies to religion. He who knows only one knows none. There are thousands of people whose faith is such that it could move mountains, who yet, if asked what religion really is, would remain silent, or would speak of outward tokens, rather than the inward nature, or of the faculty of faith."

To these scholarly testimonies I humbly subjoin: If the man who knows only the English language cannot trace the etymological derivations of its verbs, nouns and adjectives, the believer who knows only the Christian religion cannot trace its primitive source without extending his inquiries into all antedated Revelations.

If it be true, as the late Michelet affirms, that India was the original matrix of the world, the source of races, ideas, languages, and religions, it behooves all believers to extend their continual researches into the origin of the Christian religion, which flings its sheen along life's pathway, and unlocks the death-barred tomb.

During many years of my checkered and truth-searching career, I have been a schismatic, and an unyielding dogmatist, standing upon creed-platforms so narrow that unguarded mis-steps often plunged me into the bewildering labyrinths of polemic theology.

In traversing the broad field of religious credenda, I am borne toweringly above the trammels of churlish bigotry, while my asperity and love of disputation are subdued, so that I now feel liberal in my views toward the multiform, contentious sectaries.*

When the underlying truth of Goethe's paradox, with the well-versed Müller's application of it to religions, suggested its profound significance, I at once betook myself to investigating all ethnical and man-cherished Revelations.

Instead of accepting unaccredited material, gleaned from ancient religions, by surface-compilers, I, with great difficulty, and considerable expense, procured literal English

* From the *Book of all Religions*, by Hayward, we learn that more than two hundred sects have sprung from the Christian religion.

translations of the works entitled as follows:

The *Zend-Avesta*, containing the four religious books of the Parsees, bequeathed to the world by the old Iranian Prophet Zoroaster, the date* of whose writings reaches a remote antiquity; the *Rig-Veda*, which gives the earliest collocation of Brahminical prayers and hymns to the Maruts, or storm-gods; the *Bhaghavad-Gita*, or Hindu New Testament, which reveals the discourses between Krishna, Arjuna, and Sanjaya; the Analects of Confucius; the Works of Mencius; the Speculations of the old Chinese philosopher Lau-tsze; the *Koran*, by Mohammed. Also the *Dhammapada, or Path of Virtue*, by Sâkya Buddha; his Life and Teachings from the Chinese Sanskrit, by Rev. Samuel Beal; the same, by Alabaster, from Siamese sources; also, the same, from the Birmese, by

---

* Elsewhere, in a note, the reader will find historic evidence of the date of the Iranian Prophet.

Bishop Bigandet, who is a Catholic Apostolic Vicar of Ava and Pegu.*

Anterior to the advent of the gentle Nazarene, there flourished in India successive generations who must have passed from earth-life without hope — with no well-born Ariel to guide them through death's dark windings, unless we concede that Krishna of Mathura, and Buddha of Kapilavastu, were their Heaven-ordained Redeemers. Can the kind-hearted Christian for a moment believe that myriads of human beings, in that far, sunny clime, will languish in Hell's drear dominions through limitless æons? The heavens gather blackness over such a thought! The Seraphim

* "Abufazl, it is said, the minister of the Emperor Akbar, could find no one to assist him in his inquiries respecting Buddhism. We possess the whole sacred canon of the Buddhists in various languages—in Pali, Sanskrit, Birmese, Siamese, Thibetan, Mongolian and Chinese—which Akbar could not obtain by threats or bribery."—*F. Max Müller.*

retire in tears from the scene! Yet, high-throned o'er the world, God smiles through the gloom!

The theory, posited by theologians, that the so-called heathen will be saved through the vicarious, retroactive atonement of Christ, is shorn of its significance when we consider the fact that there are now four hundred millions of beings throughout the vast Asian realms who have never heard his name. If the atonement is retroactive in its effects, it can only reach those who lived prior to the advent of Jesus, and held to the Jewish Scriptures, containing God-given promises of the coming of a spiritual, sin-atoning Messiah.

As a poetic outcome of lofty odes, ensouled with melodious cadences, have been hymned in honor of the Heaven-sent Nazarene, I have struck the Muse's lyre, to swell with versual numbers "the tide of song" for the wide-famed, holy Lord Buddha, son of Suddhôdana, Rajah of the royal realm of Kapilavastu, India, who flourished 553 years ere Bethlehem's star arose, and has (according to a reliable statist's computation) over four hundred millions of followers in the extended dominions of China, Birmah, Siberia, Nepaul, Ceylon, Siam, Japan, Hindustan, Thibet and Mongolia.

In versifying this difficult thesis, I have traversed a field unpathed* by the poets, and

* Close upon the eve of my finishing this poem, a Life of Buddha (*The Light of Asia, or the Great Renunciation*), by Edwin Arnold, M.A., F.R.G.S., was issued by the popular publishers of Oriental literature, Trübner & Co., London. It appears chiefly in blank verse, and contains 238 pages, 12mo. An American edition has just been published by Roberts Brothers, Boston. The following lines bespeak the exuberant diction of its "stately march of numbers":

"Which reverence
Lord Buddha kept to all his schoolmasters,
Albeit beyond their learning taught; in speech
Right gentle, yet so wise; princely of mien,

summarized, within the purview of the following biographical narrative, a truthful delineation of the life-work, ethics, and apho-

> Yet softly-mannered; modest, deferent,
> And tender-hearted, though of fearless blood;
> No bolder horseman in the youthful band
> E'er rode in gay chase the shy gazelles;
> No keener driver of the chariot
> In mimic contest scoured the palace-courts;
> Yet in mid-play the boy would ofttimes pause;
> Letting the deer pass free; would ofttimes yield
> His half-won race because the laboring steeds
> Fetched painful breath; or if his princely mates
> Saddened to lose, or if some wistful dream
> Swept o'er his thoughts. And ever with the years
> Waxed this compassionateness of our Lord,
> Even as a great tree grows from two small leaves
> To spread its shade afar; but hardly yet
> Knew the young child of sorrow, pain or tears,
> Save as strange names for things not felt by kings,
> Nor ever to be felt."
> —(Am. Ed., p. 15.)

Among the multiform encomia so lavishly bestowed upon this grand epical poem, I find none that depictures the majesty of its diction so gracefully as

risms, which lie embosomed in the canonical record of this Heaven-gifted, world-honored Oriental.

the critique rendered by the scholarly American poet Dr. Oliver Wendell Holmes, which appears in the October number of the *International Review.*

Of Mr Arnold's scholastic and linguistic attainments the reviewer says: "He has long been known as a writer of graceful verse, a translator from Sanskrit and other languages; and, as connected with the Deccan College and Univesity of Bombay, has naturally become familiar with the internal as well as the external life of India."

SAKYA BUDDHA:

His Life and Teachings.

SAKYA BUDDHA:

A Narrative of his Life and Teachings.

SECTION I.

Yon world-sown heavens were rended!
 The dream-wrapt kings uprose!
A wild uproar was blended
 With Nature's deep-heaved throes!
Then bells in chime were ringing,
 Peals rolled through surging air;
From thrones were rajahs bringing
 Bright gems beyond compare,
To crown the new-born Savior,
 Whose banner guards unfurled;

The Heaven-sent child's behavior
    Amazed a joy-flushed world. (1)

In Lumbine's bowers deep-shaded,
    The famed Crown-prince was born;
Night's queen that close pervaded
    Till smiled the gold-hued morn;
Then heard was joy-drum beating,
    And lilting arias rare,
While Indra's hosts were meeting,
    Their shrill-toned trumps to blare. (2)

To the mural-guarded harem,
    Whose gairish tower loomed high,
The royal train did bear him,
    While Devas circled nigh;

And flowers in rare profusion
   From Flora's beds were flung,
Till staid was all intrusion
   Of din from hosts among.

No minstrel's pen can blazon
   That soul-transporting scene;
The king did proudly gaze on
   His Prince and consort-queen.
O'erflushed was sire Suddhô'na
   When cast was horoscope
Of one whom all would honor
   When paths to life he'd ope,
And rive the woof the Brahmans
   Had wove to thrall the mind,
By shriving priests, or Shamans,
   Who victims strove to bind.

Along his home-born pleasures
    Time bore with noiseless tread;
The realm enhanced his treasures,
    While Hope's plumed wings were spread,
And soared to far-off regions,
    To worlds where spirits roam—
Where dwell angelic legions,
    Who guide earth's pilgrims home.

*   *   *   *   *   *

With lore the Prince waxed stronger
    When flown had childhood's days;
He brooked at length no longer
    The siren voice of praise.
In bloom of youth's prime morning
    He whiled the light-winged hours,
Till voice 'mid-space bore warning
    To leave those sinful bowers.

Deep-versed in all the Shasters,
 And sacred tomes of yore,
He baffled languaged masters
 With words unknown before;
Outsoared in numbers stately
 The Vedic bards of old,
And conned each page sedately—
 The scroll of Fame unrolled. (3)

Embosomed long had fluttered
 A hope earth's wilds to roam;
But this he ne'er had uttered
 To friends in palace-home.
When borne on servants' shoulders,
 In gold-fringed palankeen,
He kenned the strange beholders,
 Who marked his princely mien. (4)

A sire, whose locks were hoary,
   Uprose, while gazed the crowd;
Outpoured a plaintive story,
   Then 'fore the Prince he bowed;
Alleged that pain and sorrow
   Had burdened him for years,
That death might gloom the morrow—
   Then flowed the trilling tears.

A losel, lorn, he noted,
   Who reeled athwart his way;
With dire diseases bloated,
   No antidote could stay;
Who'd laws of life neglected,
   By passion's sway o'erborne;
Deep-anguished and dejected,
   Was all of virtue shorn.

On sable bier there slumbered
 A pulseless, clay-cold form,
Whose days winged Time had numbered,
 And kin were left to mourn:
A-near the Prince stood gazing
 Long o'er that thought-reft brow;
But, what seemed more amazing,
 Was, *all* to Death must bow.

Commoved with deep-roused pity,
 The monarch-swain returned;
To leave that vice-plunged city
 His heart intensely yearned.
This god-like Oriental,
 Who wide the scepter swayed,
In mien was suave and gentle,
 By foes was undismayed.

He left the tower-crowned palace,
    The throne with gems inwrought;
With love unblent with malice,
    The grandest truths he taught.
Fair maids in roseate beauty,
    Whose soft-fringed eyes bright shone,
From sternest sense of duty
    He left to pine alone.

Some plied their arts beguiling,
    His love to still retain;
To troll, they leered when smiling;
    But glozing schemes were vain.
No woes their hearts had anguished,
    'Mong sylvan bowers they strayed;
Anon, supinely languished,
    While bickering streamlets played

'Long blooming vales, gay-dancing,
  High-hurled their water's sheen,
The ravished eye entrancing,
  While grandeur crowned the scene.

This band of high-caste sirens
  To love-wrought moods inclined,
Within great Kap'lar's 'virons,
  No more could joyance find.
From kin Siddârtha parted,
  Left crest-bowed nymphs to moan
Forlornly, dreary-hearted,
  With hope forever flown.

His parting with Rahula
  Brought many a grief - gloomed
    hour;

Time crowned his son a ruler,
    To reign with sceptered power.
His snow-white steed Kantaka
    He soon bestrode in haste— (5)
Did then his queen forsake her,
    No more home joys to taste.
The grief-whelmed Yasôdhara
    Awoke when morn smiled round,
Was warned by "shrike-tongued Mara" (6)
    The Prince could ne'er be found.
She swooning paled with sadness,
    While shone the cadent tear;
In sooth no after-gladness
    Her lonely heart could cheer. (7)

Soul-wrung was King Suddhô'na
    To learn his son had gone;

Though millions him would honor,
 Was rendered quite forlorn.
Though one would sure succeed him
 As rightful heir to throne,
Yet sorely he did need him,
 As Hope's fond dream had flown.

SECTION II.

WHAT time with argent splendor
    Pale Luna graced yon dome,
She then sad thoughts did 'gender
    In one foredoomed to roam.
He mused in silent sorrow,
    While westward rolled Night's queen;
But felt no glad to-morrow
    His soul could wholly wean
From scenes of home beclouded,
    O'ermantled deep with gloom,
And dreamland hopes enshrouded,
    Which death could ne'er entomb.

He stemmed the full-flowed Ganges
 When darkly rolled its tide; (8)
Retired near mountain-ranges,
 To roam their purlieus wide.
Long-ling'ring years he fasted
 In Pansals drear, alone; (9)
Meanwhile his thews had wasted,
 The eye but dimly shone.

A rajah's well-born daughter
 Then brought him viands rare;
Near purling rills of water,
 Her dole the Prince did share;
Which stilled the pangs of starving
 When boding death-clouds lowered;
Grand schemes he then was carving,
 With Heaven's behests empowered.

On swirls along that river
    His "golden bowl" did float,
Suggesting that forever
    'T would tides of life denote
Of souls on surges heaving,
    Who towering rise and fall,
While stern-faced Death is weaving
    A woof the scene to pall.

When ills most pestilential
    Spread gloom both far and wide,
Forethought he deemed essential
    To stay their darkling tide,
Which omened dire disaster,
    O'erwhelmed the woe-doomed race,
Who fell forsooth the faster,
    As strode grim Death apace.

Where gloom stretched wide through
    'Wela, (10)
Long years the Prince abode;
When prone 'neath lofty Sala,
    Entranced in pensive mood,
Immersed was he in thinking
    Of some device, or plan,
To lift the frail while sinking,
    And save the guilt-plunged man.

Nor gear nor pageant fashions
    Could sway his Heaven-touched soul;
He knew low-thoughted passions
    Did fiery torrents roll
Through tortured breasts while heaving,
    Disporting there with glee—
Alas! though never leaving,
    O'erwhelm them 'neath a sea,

Whose surges, like the ocean's,
　　High-toss their death-foamed spray
On shores in wild commotion,
　　To fret life's sands away.

Through sylvan glades he wandered,
　　And bosky wilds did trace;
In halcyon mood deep-pondered,
　　As rolled Time's wheels apace.
A voice from Heaven loud-sounding,
　　Soon smote the blue-tinged air;
While warders him surrounding,
　　Forth voiced a deep-felt prayer,
To rouse their Lord and Master,
　　From wolds to then withdraw;
To blazon broad each Shaster,
　　Proclaim the Heaven-sent Law. (11)

SECTION III.

What time a soft-breathed murmur
    From insects rose on air,
And smiled the green-clad Summer,
    'Long bloomy dales most fair.
He pondered then with gladness
    On scenes he highly prized;
But when emplunged in sadness,
    He thus soliloquized:

"Within this leaf-fringed wildwood,
    I'm reft of friends and home;
I mind me of my childhood,
    Of dells I once did roam,

Of fortunes left behind me,
    Of mansions towering high,
Of regal throne to bind me—
    Upswells the deep-drawn sigh

"These eerie haunts moonlighted
    I've traced at star-gemmed eve;
No gruesome gnomes affrighted
    No power can me bereave
Of new-formed hope uprising,
    That souls forlorn I'll save,
Who're truth-born laws despising,
    Though yawns the death-gloomed grave.

"O'ercloying and illusive
    Is each fast-fading thing;

Fond Hope will prove seducive
　Till life shall take its wing;
Unsphered shall be each spirit
　From cumbrous shard of clay;
Soul-rest will saints inherit,
　'Mid bowers Elysian stray.
To Fame the sage it raises
　Who delves for classic lore;
On him are lavished praises
　When heart can pulse no more.
Awards at death are meted
　To each self-cultured man;
With plaudits he'll be greeted
　By Heaven's angelic clan.

" When man has ceased progressing,
　And loses much he's learned,

A pang we feel distressing
To see his life-tide turned,
While on rude waves he's float-
ing
Bemazed and tempest-tost;
To schemes most vague devoting
His mind distraught, till lost.

"Full many a swain hath lan-
guished,
And paled 'neath passion's blight;
Full many a heart is anguished,
Engloomed with rayless night.
Like surgeful swinge of ocean,
Is borne the sin-swayed man,
In passion's wild commotion,
Till death his course shall ban.

'Earth's noblest souls have ever
    Bowed low 'neath Fortune's frown,
Whose gyves no power can sever,
    While, grief-whelmed, sinking down,
Are some who're oft neglected,
    Fate-doomed to pine alone,
And stem life's tide dejected,
    Then thrid Death's maze unknown. (12)

"Sublime is man's great Teacher,
    Yclept Dame Nature fair;
The thorn, the rose, the creature,
    She guards with equal care.
In cold her arms we'll slumber
    When earth-life blooms no more,
Though mortal flesh-forms cumber,
    Yet death-freed souls shall soar.

"From withered trunks uprising,
   The sprays have bloomed with leaves;
But, what seemed more surprising,
   While tillers gleaned the sheaves,
The leaves from young trees dying
   Were mantling o'er the ground;
A loom-gale then was sighing—
   A truth new-born smiled round.

"To live in song or story
   Must bards their ease forego, (13)
Aspire for well-earned glory,
   Breast darkling tides of woe;
Lift burdened souls low-sinking
   'Neath fell misfortune's blight:
By dint of high-aimed thinking,
   One soars to realms of light.

"From friends who've flown before us
  The grandest truths we learn;
While floats their love still o'er us,
  The Heaven-touched heart doth yearn
For home in realms supernal,
  Where gloom ne'er drowns the light;
Where dwells the King Eternal,
  High-throned 'mid star-gems bright.

"A bard through inspiration
  'Bove eyried hights can soar,
And scan the broad creation,
  Learn truths unknown before;
See light-winged spirits floating
  Through vasty realms above;
To earth-kin oft devoting
  Their aid with ceaseless love. (14)

"While siren strains so sweetly
   Float 'neath the gorgeous sky,
I fancy how completely
   They hush the rising sigh.
As gay-plumed songsters cheer me,   (15)
   With wild-toned notes that trill,
No bodings darkle near me,
   No dirge mine ear doth fill.

Wreaths wave from skies suspended,
   Flowers bloom the emerald dale,
And odors rare are blended
   Which load the sighing gale,
Outbreathed from roses blushing,
   Whose tints enchant the eye;
Heaven's arch the sun is flushing!
   Clouds fringe the verge of sky!

"On wilding syrts of meadow,
   While gathering light dews dance,
I roam 'twixt sun and shadow
   Where scenes the soul entrance.
I love the full-flushed Summer,
   To hear the murmuring rill,
To greet each glad new-comer,
   While joys my bosom fill.
O 'erpowering is the splendor
   The ambient skies reveal;
Fond Hope in man they 'gender
   When dole doth o'er him steal.

"Seem mirrored clear the Seasons
   On fading, sentient life;
Reveal they cogent reasons
   Why man should e'er shun strife.

Spring emblems childhood's morning;
　Youth blooms 'neath Summer's breath;
Crowned Autumn gives Age warning;
　Wan Winter bodeth Death.

"From chasmal deeps I've risen
　Of passion's storm-roughed sea;
Long years I've pined in prison,
　I'll set Sin's pris'ners free!
While thralled are men by error,
　They closely hug their chains;
When e'er o'erborne by terror,
　They cowering blench from pains.

"Impassioned Youth is goaded
　By scenes of madding strife,

While ermined Age is loaded
   With care through waning life.
'Tis 'lone by self-denials
   Immortal deeds are wrought;
Though gloomed is life by trials,
   With guerdons big 'tis fraught.

"Where light and warmth ne'er reigneth,
   To life the grave-worms spring,
And thrive while form remaineth,
   And then their own take wing
Through earth's evolving changes,
   True-wrought by Nature's scheme—
This thought-field man e'er ranges,
   Till lost in pensive dream.

"With graves the land is billowed,
    Ills lurk in every place;
When earth our heads hath pillowed,
    Light forms freed souls shall grace.
With woe man's life is surging,
    Like ocean's foam-wreathed waves;
To Yama's Maelstrom verging—
    'Neath passion's fire he raves.

"Death's dark-palled couch is dinted
    By fairest vestal forms,
Whose cheeks have bloomed rose-tinted,
    Suffused with glowing charms;
Which clear reveals how fleeting
    Is e'er all mundane life,
'Gainst which rude storms are beating,
    And pains and ills are rife.

"The death-god sports with mortals,
 Dread evils trail behind!
Unbarred are his huge portals,
 That pass must human-kind;
But I'll estop all sorrow,
 Sin's tidal-surge of woes;
Should Hell-fiends arm to-morrow,
 I'd front those dark-browed foes!"

SECTION IV.

The storm-clouds soon did gather,
    Wide-palled the welkin's face,
Portending wildest weather,
    While thunders rolled apace.
The fitful blasts careering
    Bowed low the Sala's crest;
The heavens wide-flamed appearing—
    The storm-gods laughed with zest;
Anon, the swift-forked lightning
    A-danced athwart the sky;
No forces round him tight'ning
    Did cause a deep-drawn sigh.

In Pansal sought he shelter,
  While raved the cloud-wrapt storm;
On moss-fringed couch did welter
  Through long night-tide till morn;
Then darkled on his vision
  Weird scenes of coming strife,
Which mocked in wild derision,
  As Mâra sought his life;
But Indra him protected,
  Repelled the puissant foes;
His life had been perfected
  Through penance and repose.

When forth he stately sallied,
  Hell's missiles straight were hurled;
With virile thews he rallied
  To save a woe-doomed world. (16)

He met King Bimbasâra
  En route for famed Benares,
Who joined him as wayfarer,
  Disburd'ning him of cares.
When reached was that great city,
  The eye full-flowed with tears;
The Fakirs roused his pity
  When flung they taunts and jeers;
But there the Master founded
  His grand truth-gloried cause;
Through realms his fame resounded,
  Profound were all his laws!

He 'leged that e'en repentance
  From sin could none absolve;
That God's unbending sentence
  In gloom would man involve,

From which no shrive could save him,
   Nor stay the tide of woes;
That passion's surge would lave him,
   Till whelmed 'neath lethal throes,
Unless by long abstention
   A well-wrought life secured,
And ceased fore'er contention
   With those to crime inured.

He oft was heard bemoaning
   That sin enthralled the mind;
No blood for crimes atoning
   He shed to save mankind;
But voiced in lucid manner,
   If passions were subdued,
The soul would reach Nirvâna, (17)
   Where woe-wails ne'er intrude.

"Lend aid betime to others,
  Your gifts 'mong poor bestrew;
Be kind to all as brothers,
  In Friendship's bonds prove true.
When e'er an o'ergloomed mortal
  Doth plain 'neath blighting care,
Fling wide the strong-hinged portal,
  Your home then let him share.

"Ne'er mind if e'en thy neighbor
  Of gold should have galore,
And thou art doomed to labor,
  Depressed by trials sore.
While shroffs are wealth amassing,
  They dwarf the godlike mind;
But strange it seems surpassing
  That gold should mortals blind.

"To fragile, luring fashions
  The prideful swain e'er yields;
While lashed by fiery passions,
  He treads o'er death-sown fields.
Ah, me! what dire diseases
  Blight fairest forms of clay!
The gem the eye most pleases,
  Time dims its sheen for aye.

"If man ignores provision
  In youth for toil-worn age,
He'll meet with cold derision
  From e'en the stoic sage;
And bale will sure betide him,
  O'erwhelm with deep despair,
While purse-proud churls will chide him,
  Misfortunes him o'erbear." (18)

He taught each staid believer
 The lord to be of self;
To yield to no deceiver,
 Nor strive for sordid pelf;
That man should be reflective,
 Scan peerless truth-gems bright,
Till loom on his perspective
 Resplendent worlds of light.

He banned the use of drinking
 Of Sôma e'en a draught;
Alleged that clearly thinking
 To Heaven would incense waft. (19)
He oft dispraised all fashions
 Which maidens daft decoy;
The wild and sordid passions,
 Which base-souled lechers cloy.

No marshaled, blood-smeared legions
    His cause sublime e'er spread;
Through earth's subastral regions,
    No gore hath marked its tread. (20)
For all religions other,
    Aggressive clans have fought;
Set brother 'gainst his brother,
    Till vesture-shrouds were wrought.

He phrased sublime Commandments,
    Ensouled with germ-thoughts great,
To guide his staid attendants,
    And kings enthroned in state.
Through æons they'll wax stronger,
    Spread wide from shore to shore,
Till suns shall rise no longer!
    Moons roll through heaven no more! (21)

SECTION V.

The Chandelah and Sooder
   Were doomed by feudal caste
To bondage, but Lord Buddha
   Their fetters rived at last; (22)
But still the birth-proud Brahman
   To transmigration clings;
With this the wary Shaman
   Oft sways the sceptered kings.
No torrid clime tribes color,
   Scarce swarts a light-skinned race;
If proof you'd have still fuller,
   We'll now their beings trace

Where black and white together
  Bask 'neath a tropic sun—
'Gainst clime, or stress of weather,
  His color holds each one. (23)
How long shall caste 'mong races
  With gyves frail mortals bind?
The serfs have left their traces
  In blood-marks deep behind.

From ooze upheaved by ocean,
  Perchance earth-life first sprung;
The theory false, or notion,
  Of which have ancients sung,
That man was erst created,
  And formed from dust of ground,
In sooth is now berated
  By scholars most profound.

The bard was deemed nigh frantic
    Who boldly once assumed,
" Where rolls the broad Atlantic,
    Wide continents have bloomed." (24)
Earth reels 'neath shocks and changes!
    Upheaves a fiery spray! (25)
Through vast creation's changes,
    God holds o'erpowering sway!

Ere formed was man or nation
    Of which famed Moses sings,
Or rose the vast creation,
    Time waved his eyas wings.
When 'merged from deeps of quiet,
    All power did God assume,
Forth issued then his fiat,
    Made earth primordial bloom.

Man copes with death-blanched Winter,
    When rave the wildest storms;
Then Nature's powers concenter,
    Engend'ring wondrous forms,
Which forth new-born come teeming,
    When flowering Spring smiles round;
Though life had long seemed dreaming
    'Neath brumal blight o'er ground.
Where blooms the Orient Summer,
    How changed the scene is there!
While floats a drowsy murmur
    Of insect-life through air.

When Sung-Yun and Fah-Hian (26)
    A pilgrimage once made,
From China's walls to Siam,
    Where waved the Bo-tree's shade,

Saw forms of footsteps molded,
  Where rose a towering mound;
Which fact they soon unfolded
  To cloistered monks profound.
'T is 'leged by ethnic sages,
  This Prince of giant-mind,
On firm-set rocks of ages,
  Left footprints bold behind; (27)
'T is clear those pilgrims noted,
  Who left their sea-laved strand,
Their lives to Buddh' devoted,
  Whose cause o'erspread the land.

The wide-famed Zoroaster,
  Whom Parsees all adore,
Was once a deep-versed Master,
  And taught as none before;

Who long preceded Moses (28)
    In founding his great cause—
The mart-bred Jew opposes
    His soul-inspiring laws.
'Mong Hindoos now are living
    This famed archaic sect,
Whose code is Mobed's giving,
    Forth calling high respect. (29)

When kernelike, vile marauders
    Robbed India long ago,
O'errunning her vast borders,
    While trailed most direful woe,
The Moslems them abetted,
    Like lions foraged bold;
To Hindoos they're indebted
    For filching once their gold. (30)

Those heathen have been plundered
 By e'en the Christian world,
Whose cannons flamed and thundered,
 Projectiles wildly hurled. (31)
As famines fell beset them,
 Death smites with giant hand;
May England ne'er forget them!
 Woe glooms that wealth-famed land!

SECTION VI.

GREAT Heber hymned in kindness
    The ode that's world-wide known—
How "heathen in their blindness
    Bow down to wood and stone."
Ne'er mortal more mistaken,
    For none on India's shore
His God has e'er forsaken,
    To idols false adore. (32)
How misconceived the notion
    That Hindoos in their zeal,
Or e'en in grave devotion,
    Should holy rev'rence feel

For idols man-created,
    Which bear no conscious sway—
Their love for God be sated
    With crass-wrought forms of clay.
Such emblems clear betoken
    That Brahm' is always nigh;
Whene'er his laws they've broken,
    Upheaves the soul-felt sigh.

That land whence all religions,
    All dialects first sprung;
From thence to gelid regions
    A dazing sheen they've flung. (33)
Such lore through vast dominions
    Sets free the trammeled mind,
And borne on lightning's pinions,
    Illumes all human-kind.

We sing of Greenland's mountains,
  Of India's coral strand,
Of Afric's golden fountains—
  The pæan ne'er will stand
The rigid test of reason,
  Whose whelming stress we ply;
It's pealed through fanes a season,
  In Lethe's shade 't will die!

Earth teems with countless billions,
  Of Christ who've never heard;
To punish one, or millions,
  Indeed 't would be absurd!
Great Heaven! the good All-father
  Will ne'er the heathen damn;
Believe had I much rather
  All priest-wrought creeds are sham!

This pride-puffed, all-wise nation
    Boasts wondrous march of mind;
Withholds all veneration
    For ages left behind.
I've e'er in sooth regretted
    That moderns weakness show;
To pagans they're indebted
    For all of God they know! (34)

The tribal nomads sordid
    Of ancient Jewish clans
Assume they first recorded
    God's soul-redemptive plans.
In torrid climes then dwelling
    Were tribes who'd never heard
Of seers 'gainst God rebelling,
    Though taught 'tis in his Word. (35)

No youth with zeal impassioned
  Truth's banner e'er unfurled,
Nor roused by schemes well-fashioned
  A slumb'rous church, or world.
Long years, with wealth of learning
  It needs creed-forms to scan;
The self-taught sage while yearning
  For light will lead the van.

He knows not one religion,
  The man who knows but one;
In thought's vast, bournless region
  The search he's just begun.
Though false to many a scholar
  This paradox may seem,
But not to languaged Müller,
  With like whose volumes teem.

He's rendered close translations,
From Sanskrit obsolete,
The works of Orient nations,
Both matchless and complete.
His pond'rous tomes have brought me
From Error's mazy way;
Soul-rousing truths they've taught me,
Which glow with keenest ray!

SECTION VII.

As Krishna of Mathura (36)
  Had once grand ethics taught,
The Lord Buddh' felt the surer ·
  His laws with truths were fraught;
That on they'd spread forever,
  Leave deep their trace behind;
All mental gyves would sever,
  Which long had thralled mankind.

I've conned Milesian fables,
  Romaunts of olden times;
With ease which me enables
  To sketch with flowing rhymes

The Lord who ne'er was thwarted
　　In deep-laid schemes or plans—
His laws have been distorted,
　　Reviled by fleering clans.

He flourished long anterior
　　To the godlike Nazarene;
Is deemed by some superior
　　In lore, if not in mien;
The truth of which I'll never
　　Assume, or e'en decide;
They'll both live on forever—
　　In hearts they'll sure abide!

The "sheep" Christ once elected
　　In mansions dwell on high;

The "goats" he then rejected
    In gloom heave many a sigh—
O'erwhelmed with lethal anguish,
    O'erawed by hostile foes;
In exile doomed to languish
    With no surcease of woes. (37)

When mordant priests of Brahma
    Assailed the Lord at length,
On thesis styled Nirvâna
    He coped with mental strength;
Averred that self-denial
    Would lift the burdened soul,
Whene'er o'erborne by trial,
    And surges o'er it roll.
The Llama throned at Thibet (38)
    Spreads wide his Master's cause,

And staidly doth exhibit
  His Heaven-inspired laws:
Which code of matchless morals
  The Ethnics highly prize;
It's won him Fame's proud laurels,
  A home in astral skies.

Where smiled the banks of 'Noma,
  He whiled the swift-winged hours;
Mandaras breathed aroma
  In garths y-prankt with flowers.
His mind in self-wrought splendor
  'Bove Fakirs' towering rose;
With flexile cadence tender
  Did laws profound disclose,
Which bore the "wheel," slow-turn-
    ing (39)
  Through all that caste swayed realm;

With love intensely burning
  He seized the swayful helm
To guide the ship while tossing (40)
  On life's wide-weltering surge,
Which loomed while she was crossing
  Death's gulf near Heaven's verge.

Along that winding river
  Whose marge was fringed with trees,
Wide-roamed the great Law-giver,
  Whose tenets seemed to please
The cowled monks world-secluded
  Through stormful scenes of life—
Saved foes who'd been deluded
  By wild uproar of strife.

Regaled with odors floating,
    He culled ambrosial flowers;
To themes sublime devoting
    His wondrous godlike powers.
The wind-swung bowers while thridding,
    Life danced with pleasaunce gay;
His eye naught smote forbidding,
    As flung Hope's star its ray.

What time light mists were falling,
    On rolled Night's wheels apace,
And gloom waxed most appalling,
    Then veiled was Nature's face;
A voice he heard low-speaking
    (While opening heavens dispread) (41)

Of truths he'd long been seeking
From earth's departed dead,
Who tidings bore, revealing
Things mortals ne'er had learned—
On volant vans swift-wheeling,
To radiant realms returned.

In life's wide, storm-vexed ocean,
Where death-foamed billows rise,
And sport in wild commotion,
A flowering island lies,
Where spirit-guides most timely
Uplift the care-bowed man;
While heaven o'ertowers sublimely,
Yon star-sown vault he'll scan.
Oft many a sage arises
By aid from spirit-world;

Oft many a dolt despises
    Till down to ruin hurled.
Ill-starred is that lorn being
    Who'll stark close eyes and ears
His earth-flown friends from seeing,
    And fling his railing sneers.

In realms that know no Summer,
    Nor fields nor blossoms fair;
Engloomed like drear Gehenna, (42)
    He'll æons languish there,
With fiends who truth once slighted,
    Till Hope's star glowed in vain;
Alas! woe-plunged, benighted!
    In thrall he'll e'er remain! (43)

SECTION VIII.

IN towering fanes of Krishna, (44)
    That kissed the gorgeous clouds,
To swell the praise of Vishnu,
    Once gathered saintly crowds.
The Lord Buddh' him succeeded,
    And sagely taught mankind;
The world profoundly needed
    His wealth of thought-throned mind.

Antique was his religion
    Ere Beth'lem's star arose;
Though zoned in that far region,
    It still sublimely grows. (45)

Vast legions now adore him
   With love that's most sublime;
In fanes they bow before him,
   Where blooms that floral clime.

A stance he held befitting,
   Grand truths to teach mankind,
While brilliant thoughts were flitting
   As lightning through the mind.
With Mâra's cohorts fighting,
   Won bays he two-score years;
His life revealed through writing
   To all sublime appears.

The world hath crowned Redeemers (46)
   Ere death did Christ betide;

Unlike all puerile dreamers,
  They've laws extended wide.
The Lord Buddh' was the true one,
  The Ariel grand of yore!
With mind-wealth 't will endue one
  His tomes to scan for lore.

I'll cling to this All-savior,
  While borne on life's wide sea!
And hope by staid behavior
  From thrall he'll set me free—
Bestow his promised guerdon
  In Heaven's eternal day;
I fain would bear a burden
  His cause to spread for aye.
From life's lone vale he's brought me
  To blaze his fame with song;

Profound are laws he's taught me,
   In faith I'm waxing strong! (47)

When forth he strolled one ev'ning,
   A youth o'ergloomed he met, (48)
Distraught with soul-pierced griev-
   ing
For one she'd ne'er forget.
"Earth's dead," he 'leged, "are
   many,
   The living are but few;
Exempt from death are n't any,
   Each bids dear friends adieu.
In yon star-gloried Heaven
   The loved and lost will meet;
Your anguished heart, though riven,
   The child again you'll greet."

'Mong graves embloomed I've wandered,
 From life's gay scenes have fled;
In sad-tuned mood deep-pondered
 Long o'er the soul-flown dead.
When once most sorely worried,
 At Night's deep noon, alone,
In hands with worn face buried,
 What time the queen-moon shone,
I thought of his vast learning—
 How world-wide famed was he,
And felt intensive yearning
 His light-robed form to see.
In vine-wreathed bower while kneeling,
 With mien surpassing fair,
Mine eye he passed swift-wheeling,
 Then heavenward soared through
  air. (49)

In spire-crowned fanes where kneeling
    The Hindoos oft were seen,
He there was heard revealing
    The law with stately mien.
With voice soft-toned as Brahma's,
    Of which have minstrels sung;
His most engaging manners
    O'er all enchantment flung.

To realms this Sage ascended, (50)
    Where gloom ne'er drowns the day;
By Indra's host attended,
    Who winged their easy way.
While long he there was living
    'Mid bloom of bowery spheres,
His law he then was giving
    To all the white-robed Seers.

When 'gain to earth returning,
 His last great work renewed;
For souls felt deepest yearning,
 With godlike gifts endued.
With eye serenely rolling,
 He scanned the ways of men;
Bore tidings most consoling
 To lift one now and then
From deeps of drear desponding,
 While lashed by passion's goad,
From virtue's path absconding,
 Till lost on Death's wide road.

His fame now reaches Heaven!
 Hell's baleful bower beneath!
Soul-lifting truths he's given,
 Quaint maxims did bequeath.

Effete creed-forms are dying,
    O'errolls them Lethe's wave;
For life are theorists sighing
    Which blooms beyond the grave.

To limn this well-starred Ariel
    Now fails my mortal pen;
To soar to worlds sidereal,
    Beyond the scope of ken,
My Muse hath callow pinions,
    And dares no lofty flight;
But gropes in earth's dominions,
    'Neath Fortune's bloom or blight.

Through flown decades he'd noted
    Wild scenes of horrent strife;

His storm-beat bark then floated
  Down foam-flecked tides of life,
Which fretted shores were lashing
  With mantling drifts of spray;
In fiendish glee were dashing
  With bold, gigantic sway. (51)

In rose-wreathed bowers of Malla,
  'Mid weird-lit vistas rare,
While prone 'neath towering Sala,
  He voiced a deep-toned prayer.
The death-god him was nearing,
  The film-touched eye to close;
When shorn of sight and hearing,
  He swooned in life's last throes.
Soul-tranced this clay-robed mortal
  On couch supine did lie,

Till wide was flung Death's portal,
   Then soared to worlds most high.
A woe-bowed host assembled,
   Whose wails through air forth pealed;
Earth widly rocked and trembled,
   Mount Meru tottering reeled! (52)

ANNOTATIONS.

(1.)

THE Grand Being's miraculous conception and birth were accompanied by convulsions in Nature, and prodigies in the skies.

When the auspicious babe was born of Queen Mâya, "a minister in state named Basita, in company with distinguished Brahmans, visited the garden of Lumbini. While there convened, Basita addressed the ministers and said: 'Do you perceive how the great earth is rocked like a ship borne over the waves? See how the sun and moon are darkened of their light; just as the stars of night in their appearance! See how all the trees are blossoming, as if the season had come—listen! there is a roll of thunder! and though there be no clouds, yet the soft rain is falling; so beautifully fertilizing in its qualities! and the air is moved by a gentle and cool breeze coming from the eight quarters—and hark to the sound of that music of Brahma, so sweetly melodious in the air! and all the Devas chanting their hymns and praises! while flowers and sweet unguents rain down through the void!'

"Such were some of the prodigies which appeared when the King, the Descendant of Mighty Conquerors; the Holy Grand Man, the Highest Crown; the Perfection of All Power; the Infinitely Meritorious Lord, excelling all—descended from the Tushita heavens, and was conceived in the world of men."—*Beal's* and *Alabaster's Life of Buddha*, conjoined.

(2.)

"Indra is the king of angels. His palace is in the second tier of heavens, reckoning from the earth, called Dawadungsa. There the thousand-eyed Lord, as he is called, is attended by myriads of angels. His charger is the three-headed elephant Erawan, and his great weapon the disk Chakra, with which he drives from heaven the fallen angels Asura. Among other treasures, he has for a trumpet a huge chank-shell, of the kind still held precious by Eastern kings.

"No Hindoo deity, unless it be the great Brahma himself, is so frequently introduced in the Siamese legends as is Indra, to whose inspiration they attribute one of their oldest books on the principles of the law."—*Alabaster*.

(3.)

The Prince on entering school confounded his teacher Visvamitra, the same as Jesus did Zaccheus, the schoolmaster at Jerusalem. There is a striking similarity in the account of Jesus given in the Apochryphal New Testament and the one given by the biographers of Buddha.*

It is said that while Visvamitra stood abashed in the presence of the marvelous child, there came from the Tushita heavens a certain Deva, accompanied by countless other Devas, and chanted this song:

> "Whatever arts there are in the world,
> Whatever Sutras and Shasters,
> This child is thorough acquainted with all,
> And is able to teach them to others."

. . . .

The Deva having finished this hymn, showered down on the Prince every sort of flower, and returned to his abode. The historic record of the early career of the Prince is so diffuse that lack of space will only allow a summarized account to be cited. I will add, *en*

---

* On this subject Bishop Bigandet says: "In reading the particulars of the life of the last Buddha, Gautama, it is impossible not to feel reminded of many circumstances relating to our Savior's life, such as it has been sketched out by the Evangelists."

passant, that the youth, with his precocious and prehensile mind, confounded his teachers in all sciences and competitive exercises.

(4.)

History informs us that when the Prince first visited the pleasure-garden of Lumbini, his stately majesty and exceeding beauty evoked from the spectators the wildest enthusiasm.

(5.)

When the horoscope was cast by the Brahmanical soothsayers on the destiny of the Prince, it was alleged that if he should ever learn that man was doomed to old age, sickness, disease, and death, he would withdraw from the palace, and become a religious ascetic. Accordingly, King Suddhôdana used every precaution to prevent his ever coming in contact with such dread evils; but when the Prince was permitted to visit the pleasure-gardens, on his way he saw them all in their direst forms.

After returning to the palace, a voice came from Space exhorting him to flee from that high-viced city to some sylvan retreat.

"Before leaving the palace, a bevy of lovely and fascinating girls surrounded him, striving, by dancing, music and songs, to attract his thoughts to pleasure; but all their enticements were vain. He now no longer found satisfaction in such things, and, heeding them not, he soon fell asleep. Then Indra, exerting his miraculous powers, caused these ladies to sleep in a most unseemly manner, quite different to that usual with ladies of high birth and good education. Some of them snored loudly; others lay with their mouths wide open; others gnashed their teeth; others rolled about in ungraceful attitudes. When the Grand Being awoke, and looked around, his heart sank within him. He conceived a disgust for worldly life, and regarded his royal palace full of lovely women as a cemetery full of horrid corpses.

The more he looked, the more sorrowful he became—the more his heart quaked for the miseries of circling existence."

Moved by such sights, he determined to lead a religious life without delay. At midnight's deepening gloom, he mounted his royal steed Kantaka, and was borne from the sinful haunts of that grand emporium, whose massive gates silently self-opened.

At dawn's first faint flush, he reached the smiling banks of the Nairanjana river, whose turbulent waters rolled near the fringe of a stately forest, where legions of angels greeted him with songs of ravishing sweetness.

He then made the following resolution: "Rather would I have my body crushed by a rock, rather would I drink the deadliest poison, or starve myself to death, than not to fulfil my vow to save all flesh from the fearful ocean of birth and death." . . .

(6.)

"Mâra is the god of love, and of death. Though this king plays the part of our Satan the tempter, he and his hosts were formerly great almsgivers, which led to their being in the highest Deva heavens, there to live nine thousand millions of years, surrounded by all the luxuries of sensuality. From this heaven the filthy one, as the Siamese describe him, descends to the earth to tempt and excite to evil."—*Alabaster*.

(7.)

As a marked episode in the career of Buddha transpired in connection with his parting with his Princess-consort, I will state that Yasôdhara had borne him a son named Rahula.

Some writers have censured the Prince for leaving home and kindred to become a religious teacher; but let it be remembered that his family was dowered with the affluence of the kingdom. To accomplish his great work of founding his sublime religion, he was compelled to withdraw from the sinful surroundings of the palace, and retire to the wilds of a forest.

(8.)

In Beal's Life of Buddha appears the following sketch of his once making an ærial flight over the sacred Ganges: "He said to the boatman, 'Pray, take me over the river.' To whom the boatman replied, 'If you can pay me the fare, I will willingly take you over the river.' Buddha said, 'I have no money to pay you.' To whom the boatman replied, 'This is the only means I have of a livelihood for my wife and children.' At this moment a flock of wild-geese flew over the Ganges. Then said the world-honored one, 'How did those geese cross the Ganges?' The boatman replied, 'By their inherent power of flying.' 'So I, by my inherent, spiritual power, will cross the Ganges, though the south bank tower higher than Mount Meru.' Then, by inherent, spiritual power, he passed over the Ganges. Continuing his flight to Benares, he alighted among the Rishis, founded his religion, and thousands of the citizens espoused his cause."

If the reader regards this miracle as improbable, or impossible, he should remember that Jesus is represented as having once walked upon the storm-roughed sea of Genesareth. (Matt. xiv, 24, *et seq.*)

(9.)

A Pansal is a "leafy hut, or sheltered abode."

(10.)

In the forest Uruwela, near the banks of the Nairanjana river, the Prince Siddârtha lived a hermit-like life, doing penance six years amid bowery shades, withdrawn from society and endeared friends.

(11.)

"Whilst the world-honored one has arrived at perfect wisdom, he has acquired that unequaled Law; he has become perfectly enlightened, and yet he has suddenly resolved on Aranya as a place of abode, and not to declare his Law for the good of men! Oh, let us exhort him not to act thus! be not thus, O world-honored one! but, for the sake of men sunk in sin, declare thy Law!" . . .

(12.)

The struggle of a hard-moiling man with overbearing Poverty, to reach "Fame's proud Temple," is finely pictured in the following Spencerian stanza:

"Ah! who can tell how hard it is to climb
  The steep where Fame's proud Temple shines afar;
Ah! who can tell how many a soul sublime
  Has felt the influence of malignant star,
  And waged with Fortune an eternal war;

Checked by the scoff of Pride, by Envy's frown,
And Poverty's unconquerable bar;
In life's lone vale remote has pined alone,
Then dropt into the grave, unpitied and unknown!"
—*Dr. Beattie.*

(13.)

The theory, posited by Goethe and Carlyle, that no great work was ever effected without renunciation and self-elevation, is clearly revealed in the teachings of Lord Buddha. Nothing so demoralizes mankind as luxury and indolence:

"For sluggard's brow the laurel never grows,
Renown is not the child of indolent Repose."
—*Thomson.*

(14.)

An atheistic lady of considerable culture was once bereft of an only daughter, who bloomed in all the radiance of youth, whose voice was as musical as the notes of a nightingale. Once, at midnight's solemn repose, she was awakened by the plaintive accents of her child, who had returned to her desolate abode to convince her skeptical mother of the continued existence of earth-flown mortals. After stemming the sullen waters of cheerless atheism (which offers no hope, but is an eternal negation), she reached the child at the door, where, in the cold, she had long waited her coming. Then the true-hearted mother (in the vision) bore the child in her loving arms to a cheerful, well-lighted room, and was overpoweringly convinced of her materialized ipseity, or selfhood:

"In spirit-form complete,
   She comes to meet her;
She stays her hurrying feet,
   Her whispers greet her;
Touch of her shadowy palms
   Stills all life's fever;
Hinting what restful calms
   Are hers forever."

(15.)

The most canorous and clear-toned songster in India is the beautiful Kalibinka. It is regarded by the natives with as much favor as the nightingale is in Europe, or the mavis or song-thrush in America.

(16.)

This terrific thunder-storm took place in the forest Uruwela. Mâra and his host had long striven to circumvent our Lord in his struggles to obtain final deliverance from the warring passions, and are represented as having caused this tempestuous storm; but they were overpowered and discomfited by Indra's mighty forces.

(17.)

I give the following views of some of the most eminent Sanskrit scholars touching this mooted, oft-perverted subject: "Numerous writers on Buddhism, in their lectures and articles, tell us that Nirvâna means annihilation, and the non-existence of the soul. This statement is more easily made than proved.

It would be better, at best, if it was not so frequently repeated in the face of contrary statements made by those well able to judge respecting the matter."—*Beal.*

"Whatever Nirvâna may be, the Siamese Buddhists assume it to be more desirable than any thing they can define as existence, and the question they raise is not 'How shall it be defined? but how can it be obtained?'"—*Alabaster.*

No writer has made this subject so clear to me as the erudite Max Müller: "I go even farther, and maintain that, if we look in the *Dhammapada,* at every passage where Nirvâna is mentioned, there is not one word which would require that its meaning should be annihilation; while most, if not all, would become perfectly unintelligible if we assigned to the word Nirvâna the meaning which it has in the metaphysical position of the canon. What does Buddha mean when he calls reflection the path to immortality, thoughtlessness the path of death. Buddhagosha does not hesitate to explain immortality by Nirvâna; and that the same idea was connected with it in the mind of Buddha is clearly proved by a passage immediately following (v, 237): 'The wise people, meditative, steady, always possessed of strong powers, attain to Nirvâna, the highest happiness.' . . .

"If the goal at which the followers of Buddha have to aim had been in the mind of Buddha perfect annihilation, 'amata,' i. e., immortality, would have been the very last word he could have chosen as its name."

(18.)

"Men who have not observed proper discipline, and have not gained wealth in their youth, they perish like old herons in a lake without fish.

"Men who have not observed proper discipline, and have not gained wealth in their youth, they lie like broken bones, sighing after the past."—*Buddha's Dhammapada.*

With the old Chinese philosopher, Lau-Tsze, economy was one of the three things he most highly prized. He enounces the following: "Three precious things I prize, and hold fast—*Humility, Compassion,* and *Economy.*"

(19.)

The most logical points ever made against the vice of intemperance are the following, by the Lord Buddha, in his Sutras, or sermons, translated by Alabaster, from the works of the late Rajah of Siam:

"As to the sin of drinking intoxicating things, consider! It is the cause of the heart becoming excited and overcome. By nature there is already an intoxication in man caused by desire, anger, and folly; he is already inclined to excess, and is not thoughtful of the impermanence, misery, and vanity of all things. If we stimulate this natural intoxication by drinking, it will become more daring; and if the natural inclination is to anger, anger will become excessive, and acts of violence and murder will result. Similarly with the other inclinations: The drunken man neither thinks of future retribution, nor present punishment. Again, spirituous liquors cause disease, liver disease, and short life; and the use of them, when it has become a fixed habit, cannot be dispensed with without discomfort, so that men spend all their money unprofitably in purchasing them, and, when the money is spent, become thieves and dacoits. The evil is both future and immediate." . . .

(20.)

Rev. W. H. H. Murray, the distinguished Congregational minister, in a lecture delivered in Boston, not long ago, said:

"Christian civilization might profit from

Buddhism; and New England might go to school in China and India. The underlying idea of Buddhism is a belief in the infinite capacity of the human intellect; a belief in the availing of true merit, and in the development of all the human faculties. It is not a heavy, sensual religion; but one purely rational, appealing to conscientiousness and intellect for support.

"While Old England and New England have used the rack, the cell, the dungeon, the inquisition, and thousands of implements of torture, there have been twenty-three hundred years of Buddhism with not a drop of blood in its onward march; not a groan along its pathway. It has never persecuted; never deceived the people; never practiced pious fraud; never appealed to prejudice; never used the sword. If Buddhists are heathen, are they not civilized heathen?"

To the above pointed remarks of Mr. Murray I subjoin the following from a speech delivered a few years since by the late Hon. Anson Burlingame:

"China is a land of scholars and schools; a land of books, from the smallest pamphlet up to voluminous encyclopedias. It is a land where privileges are common. It is a land without caste, for they destroyed their feudal system over two thousand years ago; and they built their grand structure of civilization on the great idea that the people are the source of power. This idea was uttered by Mencius between two and three thousand years since, and it was old when he uttered it. They make scholarship a test of merit."

(21.)

The following Five Commandments are the most concise and pointed of the Ten given by the Great Teacher:

1. "Not to destroy life.

2. "Not to obtain another's property by unjust means.

3. "Not to utter falsehood.

4. "Not to indulge the passions, so as to invade the legal, or natural, rights of other men.

5. "Not to partake of anything intoxicating."—*Alabaster*.

(22.)

In the Brahmanical system of Caste, the Chandelah, in consequence of mixed marriage, is doomed to be a wretched outcast. The Sooder, who is born from the foot of Brahma, is fated to a state of perpetual bondage to the high-caste, lordly Brahman.

This soul-enslaving system of servitude the Lord Buddha most strenuously opposed. A similar system did Jesus encounter among the stilted, crest-raised Pharisees.

The wretched fate of the unfortunate Chandelah, or Pariah, is finely portrayed in the following lines from the scholarly poet Goethe.

"We are not of noble kind,
   For with woe our lot is rife;
And what others deadly find
   Is our only source of life.
Let this be enough for men,
   Let them if they will despise us;
But thou, Brahma, thou shouldst prize us,
All are equal in thy ken."

(23.)

In the American Antiquities we find the following touching the unchangeable effects of climate on the complexions of different races:

"In torrid climes, both the white and black, with all the intermediate shades between the two extremes, are found, as also the black with curled hair in the northern regions, and in many countries of the Old World. The dark-complexioned varieties of mankind are found near the poles; as people of the *same* complexion are found over the whole continent of America, under all its various climates."

(24.)

Beattie's Minstrel.

(25.)

Near Mount Hecla, in Iceland, there is a marvelous column of boiling water thrown upward, above ninety feet, by the force of a subterranean fire.

(26.)

Travels of Fah-Hian and Sung-Yun, Buddhist Pilgrims, from China to India (400-518 A.D.), *by S. Beal.*

(27.)

"Fah-Hian mentions two footprints in Ceylon. 'Buddah, by his spiritual power, planted one foot to the north of the royal city, and one on the top of a mountain; the distance between the two being fifteen yoganas (say a hundred miles').

"You have all heard of the two footprints sculptured on the summit of Mount Olivet, and worshiped by pilgrims as the marks left when Jesus sprang into the sky at his ascension." . . .

(28.)

Touching the date when the Iranian Prophet flourished, I quote from the writings of the well-known, scholarly author, Hudson Tuttle:

"The eminent Oriental scholar, M. Haug, places Zoroaster 4,300 B.C., thus antedating Moses. But far better are the ancient Greek writers. They agree in placing the era of Zoroaster more than 6,000 years B.C. . . .

"Hermippus, who made the books and religion of the Magi the study of his lifetime, states, according to Pliny, on the authority of Agonakes, his teacher, that Zoroaster lived about 5,000 years before the Trojan war, 6,180 B.C." . . .

The erudite A. H. Bleeck, in his Prolegomena to his English translation of the *Zend-Avesta*, from Prof. Spiegle's German, says:

"When we attempt to go farther, and fix the date of the Iranian Prophet, we are met by difficulties at present insuperable, and we can neither deny nor confirm the statement of Aristotle, who places Zoroaster 6,000 years before his own time, or, rather, that of Plato, about 360 B.C."

(29.)

A Mobed is the high-priest of the Parsees, the followers of Zoroaster.

"A small remnant of them still cling to the Persian soil; but the mass passed across the Persian Gulf into Hindostan, where they received welcome and protection from the Rajah of Guzarat.

"The Parsees of Bombay are the richest, and most prosperous, and most active, class of merchants in India, the English at Calcutta and Madras excepted. It is more due to them than to any others that Bombay has become that great center and emporium of the trade of Western India. Shrewd and industrious, they are far from being either over-reaching or parsimonious.

"The merchants of European and American cities may well emulate the commercial honesty of this race. They are also lavish on occasion with their wealth. . . . Among themselves they are rather a brotherhood than a class or race. There is a genuine Freemasonry among the Parsees, each being always ready to help his fellow, and, thus knit together, they possess that wide and strong influence which is the result of unity. It is no empty boast of theirs that throughout their community there is not a single prostitute. . . . It is rarely a Parsee is ever brought into court, either on a criminal or civic charge. Prompt in the payment of their debts, almost invariably true to their engagements, they are also quiet, orderly, and law-abiding."—*Appletons' Journal.*

(30.)

"Mahmoud, the Sultan of Ghuzni, on hearing the astonishing accounts of the relics of the pagoda of Sumnaut, whose roof was covered with plates of gold, and encircled with precious stones, besieged the place, whose inhabitants fell an easy prey before the victorious Moslems. . . . In the fury of his Mohammedan zeal against supposed idols, he smote off the nose of the image. Though large sums were offered for his desistance, he only proceeded with his soldiers to destroy it. He found an infinite variety of diamonds, rubies, and pearls, of a water so pure and a magnitude so uncommon that the soldiers were overwhelmed with astonishment. The accumulated riches of this affluent region were so immense that they exceeded the power of imagination to grasp them.

"Of this Moslem marauder, we read that when he approached the scenes of dissolution, he ordered his sacks of gold and jewels to be brought before him, that he might gaze for the last time upon his earthly treasures, then burst into tears, probably from the dismal reflection of the thousands of lives he had sacrificed to obtain them; and perhaps from the thought that they would soon pass into other hands, and he to the doom of eternity." — *W. Howitt.*

(31.)

The great injustice and cruelty of England toward those so-called heathen is most vividly depicted by Goldwin Smith—an Englishman of scholarly ability, now a resident of Canada—in a scathing criticism of the British rule in India, called out by the war with the Ameer of Cabul. We make the following extracts from Prof. Smith's criticism, as we find it quoted by Mr. G. B. Stebbins in the *Religio-Philosophical Journal:*

. . . "In every country but one, the

hearts of all who love justice and hate iniquity will be on the side of the Ameer; and, if he is beaten, he will be trodden down into the general mass of spiritless and hopeless servitude of the two hundred millions who owe their allegiance to the Empress of India— that is, to Queen Victoria."

Of the late famine in Hindostan he says: "Whether it was four millions or only a million and a quarter of these wretches who died in the late famine, nobody can exactly tell.

"People wonder that Christianity does not make more headway in Hindostan. The converts are few. Yet the religion of Christ prospers as much as it could be reasonably expected to prosper in partnership with the pride of conquest, the insolence of race, fiscal extortion and massacre. The preachers themselves are imperial. Lord Elgin found reverend gentlemen out-Heroding even lay terrorists in the ferocity of their sentiments at the time of the mutiny; and he says that, if he were to pursue a humane policy in China, the loudest outcries against him would be raised by the missionaries and the women." . . .

Miss Florence Nightingale has also written a caustic article on the cruelty of her mother-countrymen toward famine-stricken India.

(32.)

Max Müller reports the following extract from a speech of a Hindoo at Benares, delivered before an audience of natives and English, which will show that Buddhists are not idolaters:

"If by idolatry," says this Hindoo scholar, "is meant a system of worship which confines our ideas of the Deity to a mere image of clay or stone, which prevents our hearts from being expanded and elevated with lofty notions of the attributes of God—if this is what is meant by idolatry, we disclaim and abhor idolatry, and deplore the ignorance or uncharitableness of those who charge us with this groveling system of worship. We really lament the ignorance or uncharitableness of those who confound our representative worship with the Phœnician, Grecian, or Roman idolatry, as represented by European writers, and then charge us with polytheism, in the teeth of the thousands of texts in the Puranas, declaring in clear and unmistakable terms that there is but one God, who manifests himself as Brahma, Vishnu, and Siva, in his functions of creation, preservation and destruction."

Wong-Ching-Foo, a Buddhist missionary priest, in a lecture delivered in New Haven, said: "If Buddhists are idolaters, most surely are the Christians. On entering a cathedral in one of your cities, I was struck with astonishment at the sight of so many images. I asked the Catholic priest if Christians worshiped those images: to which he replied, 'None but the grossly ignorant devotee worships them. They are merely emblems of real personages which intelligent Catholics adore.'"

I will add: As Catholics bow before images in their devotions, and as they largely outnumber the Protestants, it follows by ilative reasoning that the major part of Christians are idolaters.

(33.)

The spiritual dominions of Buddha extend to Siberia, and even Swedish Lapland.

(34.)

For the behoof of all who fancy that the ancients were inferior to moderns in genius and literature, I cite the following from the poet Alexander Pope: "The ancients (to say the least of them) had as much genius as we have; and to take more pains, and to employ more time, cannot fail to produce more complete pieces. They constantly applied themselves not only to that art, but to that single branch of an art, to which their talent was most powerfully bent; and it was the business of their lives to correct and finish their works for posterity. If we can pretend to have used the same industry, let us expect the same immortality." . . .

The writer has reference to the ancient Greek poets and philosophers.

(35.)

In the American Antiquities we read that "Cavigero supposes that the nations of Aztalan came from Asia, across the Pacific, along the region of the coast of the Chinese sea and islands, reaching America not far from Bhering's Strait, and from thence followed along the coast of the Pacific, till they came, in process of time, to a milder climate.

"To this Mr. Atwater adds, and supposes them to have thence worked across the continent, as well as in other directions, as far as the regions of the Western States and Territories, where they may have lived thousands of years, as their works denote."

(36.)

This Hindoo Deity and Savior, who flourished about 950 B.C. (though positive evidence of the correctness of this epoch cannot be established),* was miraculously engendered by the god Vishnu, and born of a maiden of vestal purity, named Devanaguy, in a prison at Mathura. The canonic records of his career and teachings may be found in the Upanishads of what is called the Holy Bhagavad-Gita, or Hindoo New Testatment.

His youthful career was marked by heroic

* "That the name of Krishna, and the general outline of his story," says the learned Sir William Jones, "were long anterior to the birth of our Savior, and probably to the time of Homer, *we know very certainly*."
—*Asiatic Researches*, vol. i, p. 259.

deeds, in redressing the wrongs of humanity, while to free the oppressed never strove a worthier paladin.

To give the reader an idea of the style of this Sanskrit Philosophical Poem, I cite the following:

Arjuna thus addresses Krishna: "The universe, O Krishna! is justly delighted with thy glory, and devoted to thee. The Rákshasas flee affrighted to the divers quarters of heaven, and all the multitudes of the Siddas salute thee. And, indeed, why should they not adore thee, O great one! thee, the first creator, more important even than Brahma himself? O infinite king of gods! habitation of the universe! thou art the one indivisible, the existing and not existing, that which is supreme. Thou art first of the gods, the most ancient person. Thou art the supreme receptacle of this universe. Thou knowest all, and mayest be known, and art the supreme mansion. By thee is this

universe caused to emanate, O thou of endless forms! Air, Yama, fire, Varuna, the moon, the progenitor, and the great-grandfather (of the world) art thou. Hail! hail. to thee a thousand times! and again, yet again, hail to thee! Hail to thee from before! Hail to thee from behind! Hail to thee from all sides, too! Thou All! Of infinite power and immense might, thou comprehendest all; therefore thou art All. As I took thee merely for a friend, I beseech thee without measure to pardon whatever I may, in ignorance of this thy greatness, have said from negligence or affection, such as, 'O Krishna! O son of Yadu! O friend!' and every thing in which I may have treated thee in a joking manner, in recreation, repose, sitting, or at meals, whether in private or in the presence of these, Eternal One!
. . . . Now that I see what I have never seen before, I am delighted, and my heart is shaken with awe. Show me that other form

only, O god! Be gracious, O king of gods! habitation of the universe! With thy tiara, thy staff, and thy discus in thy hand, thus only do I desire to see thee. Invest thyself with that four-armed form, thou of a thousand arms, of every form!"

The Holy One spoke: "I have shown thee that supreme form, Arjuna! in kindness to thee by my own mystic virtue—that, which is my splendid, universal, infinite, primeval form, never yet beheld by other than thee. Not by studying the Vedas, nor by almsgiving, nor rites, nor severe mortification, can I be seen in this form, in the world of man, by other than thee, O best of the Kurus! Be not alarmed, or in a troubled condition, at having seen this so terrible form of mine. But look, free from fear, with happy heart, upon that other form only of mine, namely, this."

Sanjaya spoke: "Vásudeva, having thus addressed Arjuna, showed him again his proper form, and the Great One consoled him who was alarmed by again assuming a pleasant shape."

Arjuna spoke: "Now that I behold this thy pleasant human shape, thou who art prayed to by mortals! I am composed in my right mind, and brought back to my natural condition."

The Holy One spoke: "That form of mine which thou hast seen is very difficult to behold. Even the gods are always anxious to behold that form. Neither by studying the Vedas, nor mortification, nor almsgiving, nor sacrifice, can I be seen in such a form as thou hast seen me. But only by worship, of which I alone am the object, can I really be known and seen, Arjuna, and approached in this form, O harasser of thy foes! He who performs his actions for me, intent on me, free from interest, and from enmity toward any being, comes to me, O son of Pandu!"

(37.)

The period denoted by the Second Coming of Christ, and its associate events, is misunderstood by the Christian world. He taught his immediate disciples that his second coming would transpire during their lifetime—before the then current generation should have passed away. (Matt. xvi, 28, and xxiv. 34; Luke xvii, 30.) In Matt. xxv, 31, *et seq.*, the goats represent the God-cursed Jews, who were then doomed to everlasting punishment. They were scattered earth-wide among all nations, agreeably to Christ's prediction. They are a "taunt and a curse"; hated and despised by the whole civilized world. Limitation of space precludes further dilation upon the fulfilment of Christ's and their own prophet's veritable predictions. (Jer. xxiv, 9, *et seq.*)

(38.)

"The Delia-Llama is a name given to the sovereign pontiff, or high-priest, of the Thibetan Tartars, who resides at Patoli, in a vast palace on a mountain, on the banks of Burhampooter, a few miles from Lahassa.

"This sovereign vicegerent of the Deity on earth is never to be seen only in a secret place in his palace, amid a great number of lamps, sitting cross-legged upon a cushion, and decked with gold and precious stones; where, at a distance, the people bow themselves before him. He seldom speaks, even to the greatest princes, but only lays his hands upon their heads, and they are fully persuaded they receive from thence a full forgiveness of all their sins."—*Hayward*.

I subjoin the following: The present cultus of Buddhism bears but little similarity to its primitive status, when founded by its immortal Author. It has evidently been perverted by an imperial high-priesthood. In a manner strikingly resemblant has the Christian religion been corrupted by the all-potent decretals of the Romish prelacy.

(39.)

"*Wheel of the Law*. In this passage the Siamese author speaks of the wheel as if it was the quoit-like weapon (chakra) the emblem of the power of Indra, king of the angels, and of emperors of the world; a few lines farther on, the allusion seems to be the circle of cause and effect. Buddha is said to account for continued existence in transmigration. The twelve causes and effects are called the twelve constituent parts of the wheel."—*Alabaster*.

(40.)

"The golden junk or ship. In the Life of Buddha we read of 'the lustrous vessel of the law,' by which Buddha would enable men to cross the ocean of transmigrating existence, and reach the other shore, i. e., Nirvâna."—*Ibid*.

(41.)

The Lord Buddha at this period was so intensely spiritually-minded that he was constantly *en rapport* with the spirit-world while dwelling in his sequestered abode. Bishop Bigandet represents him as then living upon the verge of Heaven.

(42.)

A Greek phrase which is rendered Hell twelve times in the Gospels of the New Testament, and is believed by theologians to denote the regions of the lost.

(43.)

The fleering corporealist, who denies the immortality of the soul, might read with profit the following argument in its favor by Socrates, an Athenian philosopher, who flourished about 470 B.C.

The first argument which he urges is, that everything in Nature is produced or generated from its opposite. "Thus, the worse proceeds from the better, and the better from the worse. From the state of wakefulness we pass to sleep, and from sleep to wakefulness. And as from being alive we go to the dead, and so, from being dead, we enter into another life.

"The soul must subsist after death, because it existed *prior* to the present life. The soul will exist hereafter, because it is a *simple, unchanging substance.* If it were a compound, like the body, it must, like the body, be dissolved. But as it is not a compounded substance, it is not subject to mutations like the body, and the conclusion is that it will never be dissolved. It belongs to the soul to *govern* the body, and not the body the soul; which proves that the soul is allied to Divinity, and, like that, is immortal. Into whatever the soul enters it introduces *life;* which shows that life is essential to it, and that it can never be subject to the opposite of life, which is death." . . .

In all ages, have didactic bards verified the inter-communion of the soul-flown dead with earth-mortals; but none whose works I have read, excepting Thomson, has more gracefully portrayed their mission to the denizens of this mundane globe than has the polished poet Rogers in his *Pleasures of Memory:*

"Oft may the spirits of the dead descend
  To watch the silent slumbers of a friend;
  To hover round his evening-walk unseen,
  And hold sweet converse on the dusky green;
  To hail the spot where once their friendship grew,
  And Heaven and Nature opened to their view!
  Oft, when he trims the cheerful hearth, and sees
  A smiling circle emulous to please;
  There may these gentle guests delight to dwell,
  And bless the scenes they loved on earth so well."

(44.)

At Mathura and Siam can be seen fanes and pagodas with lofty spires. Alabaster describes one in Siam, whose spire reaches an altitude little less than the most towering in our largest emporiums.

(45.)

The question is often raised by Christians why Buddhism is confined almost exclusively to Asia, while the religion taught by the godlike Nazarene is widespread throughout Europe and America.

A solution of this question I give by affirming that the spread of the Christian religion is due to the following circumstances: Had Buddha been born in Judea, at the date of the appearance of Jesus, it is evident at first blush that his religion would have been founded there; and from thence through the prevailing dialects it would have spread through European nations, and subsequently have reached this hemisphere. With the tide of emigration, its course would have been westward, following the setting of the sun. Had Christ been born in India at the time of Buddha, his religion would have been founded there; and, peradventure, I should have written his biographical narrative, instead of Buddha's.

It is a singular fact, and worthy of note, that missionaries are being sent to Judea, to proclaim to the benighted denizens the glories of the religion of Jesus, in the land of his nativity.

(46.)

The world had three Redeemers before the advent of the humble Nazarene. They were: Buddha of Kapilavastu, Krishna of Hindostan, and Osiris of Egypt.

In the "Book of the Dead" (Bunsen's *Egypt*) we find an account of the crucifixion of Osiris, who flourished about 3,000 years B.C. In this antique work are found religious rituals most strikingly similar to those which are observed by Christians.

In a book now before me, entitled *The*

World's Sixteen Crucified Saviors, or Christianity Before Christ, I find this loose statement: "Buddha, Hindoo Sâkya, crucified 600 B.C."

I am neither prepared to confirm nor deny the truthfulness of many of the author's statements, yet I shall make an issue with him touching the crucifixion of Buddha. As the last note to my poem contains *full particulars* touching the death of Buddha, I refer the reader to the aforesaid note to disprove his allegation that he was crucified, and therein show that he died a natural death in the garden of the Malla Princes, hard by the city of Kusinagara.

(47.)

Many years has the writer lived unfellowed, in templed shades, within the purlieu of a rural hamlet, withdrawn from society; during which period he investigated many ancient and modern religions; but none so fully meets his approval as the one founded by the fame-crowned Ascetic of Kapilavastu, whose teachings he has endeavored to bring before the American people.

(48.)

Reference is here had to the story of Kisâgotimi, who bemoaned the loss of an only child, the account of which may be found in *Buddhagosha's Parables*. This parable is given in full in the closing paragraph of the Excursus.

(49.)

Oft has the writer, at night-tide's deepening hush, retired from the dinning haunts of his fellow-villagers, for silent self-communing in God's hallowed "Acre":

"Where spirit-forms athwart the solemn dusk
Tremendous sweep, or seem to sweep, along;
And voices more than human, through the void
Deep-sounding, seize the enthusiastic ear!"
—Thomson.

Oft, too, has he repeated the following, from the same highly-gifted poet:

" . . . . "Deep-roused, I feel
A sacred terror, a severe delight
Creep through my mortal frame; and thus methinks
A voice, than human more, the abstracted ear
Of fancy strikes: 'Be not of us afraid,
Poor kindred man! thy fellow-creatures, we
From the same Parent-Power our beings drew;
The same our Lord, and laws, and great pursuit;
Once some of us, like thee, through stormy life,
Toiled, tempest-beaten, ere we could attain
This holy calm, this harmony of mind,
Where purity and peace immingle charms.'"

(50.)

"The Modern Buddhist" alleges that the Lord Buddha disappeared for a period of three months, and preached to the spirits of the Dawadungsa world, and afterward returned to earth. The miracle he regards as a well-attested, accredited fact. He thinks the Lord could not have concealed himself from his immediate disciples, but that he really visited the spirit-world.

How strongly this reminds us of Christ, when he preached to the spirits of the Noachian generation, who were in prison in the time of Peter; but "were disobedient, when once the long-suffering of God waited, in the days of Noah, while the ark was a-preparing, wherein few, that is, eight souls, were saved by water." (I Peter, iii, 18, *et seq.*)

(51.)

"Buddha's teachings during many years were not unopposed. Failing to equal him in science and miracle-working, his opponents tried to ruin his character. They leagued with a woman to charge him with unchastity. . . They bribed her to accuse him of misconduct with her; and, when she had proclaimed her story, was murdered by her bribers, in order that Buddha might be suspected of the act.

This plan failed, for the plotters, in a drunken revel, boasted of their craft, and acknowledged their villainy."—*Alabaster*.

(52.)

The distinguished Oriental traveler, Dr. J. M. Peebles, in his annotations on the Oral Discussion between a Buddhist priest named Migettuwatte and Rev. P. Silva, an English clergyman, held at Pantura, Ceylon, says:

"The general testimony of scholars, as well as the histories of the Siamese, Birmese, and Singhalese, unite in the opinion that Sâkyamuni Gautama Buddha died a natural death, at the age of about eighty years, the event occurring during the reign of Adazathat."

He gives Bishop Bigandet's account of the final summation of his earth-career, and particulars touching his demise; but I quote the following from Alabaster's Life of Buddha:

"On reaching the city of Kusinagara, attended by his immediate disciples, he gave them final instructions. Reclining between two lofty Sala-trees, in the garden of the Malla Princes, he uttered his last words: 'All things that are earth-born are perishable; qualify yourselves for the imperishable.' Absorbed in ecstatic meditation, he remained until the third watch of the night, and then expired.

"Then there was a great earthquake; and the pious who had not the perfection of saints wept aloud with uplifted arms, and reeled about, exclaiming, 'Too soon has the blessed one expired. Too soon has the eye closed on the world.' But the more advanced in religion calmly submitted themselves, saying, 'Transitory things are perishable; in this world there is no permanence.'" *

* In the Life of Gautama Buddha, by Edwin Arnold, we read the following touching the place and date of his birth and death: "Buddha was born on the borders of Nepaul, about 620 B.C., and died 543 B.C., at Kusinagara, in Oudh."

On the authority of Max Müller, I have placed the epoch of his birth at about 553 B.C. Touching the year of Buddha's advent, there seems to be a diversity of opinion among authors; but nearly all agree that his birth was between 550 and 600 B.C.

With Alabaster, Peebles, and Bigandet, Mr. Arnold agrees that Buddha died a natural death. This corroborative and consentient testimony disproves the statement made by the author of the *World's Sixteen Crucified Saviors*, that he was crucified near the Nepaul Mountains.

EXCURSUS.

To GIVE the reader a correct view of Buddha's ethical and religious codes, as taught by him in his *Dhammapada, or Path of Virtue,*[*] I make the following citations:

[*] Translated from the Pali, by F. Max Müller. I have not numbered, or arranged in consecutive order, chapter and verse, my quotations from the *Dhammapada*. I have adopted the present course to avoid seeming repetitions, with slight variations, which plainly appear.

Houghton, Osgood & Co., the well-known publishers in Boston, have recently issued the *Dhammapada*, or the Buddhist Canon, translated from the Chinese, by Samuel Beal, B.A., Professor of Chinese in University College, London.

Although the phraseology varies considerably from Max Müller's translation from the Pali, yet the general

All that we are is the result of what we have thought; it is made up of our thoughts. If a man speaks or acts with an evil thought, pain follows, like a shadow that never leaves him.

If a man does what is good, let him do it again; let him not delight in sin; pain is the outcome of evil.

Let us live happily, then, not hating those who hate us! let us dwell free from hatred among men who hate us!

identity of both is substantially indicated. The following quotation exhibits the contrast:

"Although a man may have heretofore been careless, yet if afterward he is able to govern and restrain himself, this man becomes illustrious, or illuminates the world, and the more he reflects the more resolved will he become to use self-restraint. A man may have done many things wrong, but if he recovers himself and atones for the evil by doing good, this man becomes illustrious in the world, and the more he reflects the more virtuous he will become. A man who in the prime of life leaves his home and perfectly tutors him-

Health is the greatest of gifts, contentedness the best riches; trust is the best of relatives; Nirvâna, the highest happiness.

He who walks in the company of fools suffers a long way; company with fools, as with an enemy, is always painful; company with the wise is pleasure, like meeting with kinsfolk.

Therefore, one ought to follow the wise, the intelligent, the learned, the much-enduring, the dutiful, the elect; one ought to follow a self in the doctrine of Buddha, this man shines out in the world as the moon when it bursts from the cloud. The man who in times past has done wickedly, but afterward halts in his career and offends no more, that man shines out in the world as the moon when it emerges from the cloud."

It seems, by the wide-spread and growing interest in this ancient religion, that God is especially moving the hearts of men in Europe and America to render in English the sublime doctrines of Buddhism, which have lain buried for ages in the sand of an obsolete language.

good and wise man, as the moon follows the path of the stars.

He who does not rise when it is time to rise, who, though young and strong, is full of sloth, whose will and thoughts are weak, that lazy and idle man will never find the way to knowledge.

He who, by causing pain to others, wishes to obtain pleasure himself, he, entangled in the bonds of hatred, will never be free from hatred.

What ought to be done is neglected, what ought not to be done is done; the sins of unruly, thoughtless people are always increasing.

The disciples of Gautama (Buddha) are always well awake, and their thoughts day and night are always set on Buddha.

The hard parting, the hard living alone, the uninhabitable houses, are painful; painful is the company with men who are not our equals. . . .

Good people shine from afar, like the snowy mountains; bad people are not seen, like arrows shot by night.

He who, without ceasing, practices the duty of eating alone and sleeping alone, he, subduing himself, alone will rejoice in the destruction of all desires, as if living in a forest.

He who says what is not, goes to hell; he also who, having done a thing, and says, I have not done it. After death both are equal; they are men with evil deeds in the next world.

Four things does a reckless man gain who covets his neighbor's wife: a bad reputation, an uncomfortable bed; thirdly, punishment; and lastly, hell.

Like a well-guarded frontier fort, with defenses within and without, so let a man guard himself. Not a moment should escape, for they who allow the right moment to pass suffer pain when they are in hell.

They who are ashamed of what they ought not to be ashamed of, such men, embracing false doctrines, enter the evil path.

The Bhikshu who controls his mouth, who speaks wisely and calmly, who teaches the meaning and the Law, his word is sweet.

He who never identifies himself with his body and soul, and does not grieve over what is no more, he indeed is called a Bhikshu.

O Bhikshu, empty this boat! if emptied, it will go quickly; having cut off passion and hatred, thou wilt go to Nirvâna.

This salutary word I tell you, as many as are here come together: Dig up the root of thirst, as he who wants the sweet-scented Usira root must dig up the Birna grass, that Mâra (the tempter) may not crush you again and again, as the stream crushes the reeds.

As a tree is firm as long as its root is safe, and grows again even though it has been cut down, thus, unless the yearnings of thirst are destroyed, this pain (of life) will return again and again.

He whose desire for pleasure runs strong in the thirty-six channels, the waves will carry away that misguided man, namely, his desires which are set on passion.

The channels run everywhere, the creeper (of passion) stands sprouting; if you see the creeper springing up, cut its root by means of knowledge.

A creature's pleasures are extravagant and luxurious; sunk in lust and looking for pleasure, men undergo (again and again) birth and decay.

Men, driven on by thirst, run about like a

snared hare; held in fetters and bonds, they undergo pain for a long time, again and again.

Men, driven on by thirst, run about like a snared hare; let, therefore, the mendicant who desires passionlessness for himself drive out thirst.

He who in a country without forests (i. e., after having reached Nirvâna) gives himself over to forest life (i. e., to lust), and who, when removed from the forest (i. e., to lust), runs to the forest (i. e., to lust), look at that man! though free, he runs into bondage.

Wise people do not call that a strong fetter which is made of iron, wood, or hemp; far stronger is the care for precious stones and rings, for sons and a wife.

That fetter do wise people call strong which drags down, yields, but is difficult to undo; after having cut this at last, people enter upon their pilgrimage, free from cares, and leaving desires and pleasures behind.

Let a man leave anger, let him forsake pride, let him overcome all bondage! No sufferings befall the man who is not attached to either body or soul, and who calls nothing his own.

He who holds back rising anger like a rolling chariot, him I call a real driver; other people are but holding the reins.

Speak the truth, do not yield to anger; give, if thou art asked, from the little thou hast; by those steps thou wilt go near the gods.

He whose conquest is not conquered again, whose conquest no one in this world escapes, by what path can you lead him, the Awakened, the Omniscient, into a wrong path?

He whom no desire with its snares and poisons can lead astray, by what path can you lead him, the Awakened, the Omniscient, into a wrong path?

Even the gods envy those who are awakened and not forgetful, who are given to meditation, who are wise, and who delight in the repose of retirement (from the world).

Hard is the conception of men, hard is the life of mortals, hard is the hearing of the True Law, hard is the birth of the Awakened (the attainment of Buddhahood).

Not to commit any sin; to do good, and to purify one's mind—that is the teaching of the Awakened.

The Awakened call patience the highest penance, long-suffering the highest Nirvâna; for he is not an anchorite who strikes others, he is not an ascetic (Shramna) who insults others.

Not to blame, not to strike, to live restrained under the law, to be moderate in eating, to sleep and eat alone, and to dwell on the highest thoughts—this is the teaching of the Awakened.

Men driven by fear go to many a refuge—to mountains and forests, to groves and sacred trees.

But that is not a safe refuge, that is not the best refuge; a man is not delivered from all pains after having gone to that refuge.

He who takes refuge with Buddha, the Law, and the Church; he who, with clear understanding, sees the four holy truths:

Namely, pain, the origin of pain, the destruction of pain, and the eight-fold holy way that leads to the quieting of pain—

That is the safe refuge, that is the best refuge; having gone to that refuge, a man is delivered from all pain.

A supernatural person is not easily found; he is not born everywhere. Wherever such a sage is born, that race prospers.

Happy is the arising of the Awakened, happy is the teaching of the True Law, happy is the peace of the Church, happy is the devotion of those who are at peace.

He who pays homage to those who deserve homage, whether the Awakened (Buddha) or his disciples; those who have overcome the host (of evils), and crossed the flood of sorrow; he who pays homage to such as have found deliverance and know no fear—his merit can never be measured by anybody.

He who lives looking for pleasures only, his senses uncontrolled, immoderate in his enjoyments, idle and weak, Mâra (the tempter) will certainly overcome him, as the wind throws down a weak tree.

As rain does not break through a well-thatched house, passion will not break through a well-reflecting mind.

The virtuous man is happy in this world, and he is happy in the next; he is happy in both. He is happy when he thinks of the good he has done; he is still more happy when going on the good path.

The thoughtless man, even if he can recite a large portion (of the law), but is not a doer of it, has no part in the priesthood, but is like a cowherd counting the cows of others.

Reflection is the path to immortality; thoughtlessness, the path of death. Those who reflect do not die; those who are thoughtless are as if dead already.

Follow not after vanity, nor after the enjoyment of love and lust! He who reflects and meditates obtains ample joy.

Not a mother, not a father, will do so much, nor any other relative; a well-directed mind will do us greater service.

He who knows that his body is like froth, and has learnt that it is as unsubstantial as a mirage, will break the flower-pointed arrow of Mâra, and never see the King of Death.

Death carries off a man who is gathering flowers, and whose mind is distracted, as a flood carries off a sleeping village.

Hatred does not cease by hatred at any time; hatred ceases by love; this is an old rule.

What is the use of platted hair, O fool! what of the raiment of goatskins? Within thee there is ravening, but the outside thou makest clean.*

He whose evil deeds are covered by good deeds brightens up this world like the moon when she rises from behind the clouds.

As the bee collects honey and departs without injuring the flower, so let the sage dwell on earth.

*Most strikingly parallelistic are some of the phrases in this passage with the following: "Ye make clean the outside of the cup and the platter, but within are full of extortion and excess." (Matt. xxiii, 25.)

Let no man think lightly of good, saying in his heart, It will not benefit me. Even by the falling of water-drops a water-pot is filled.

Long is the night to him who is awake; long is a mile to him who is tired; long is life to the foolish, who does not know the true law.

If a traveler does not meet with one who is his better, or equal, let him firmly keep to his solitary journey; there is no companionship with a fool.

If an intelligent man be associated for one minute only with a wise man, he will soon perceive the truth, as the tongue perceives the taste of soup.

Fools of little understanding have themselves for their greatest enemies; for they do deeds which must bear bitter fruit.

If you see an intelligent man who tells you where true treasures are to be found, who shows what is to be avoided, and who administers reproof, follow that wise man; it will be better, not worse, for those who follow him.

There is no suffering for him who has abandoned grief, and finished his journey; who has freed himself from all desires, and thrown off all fetters.

They who have riches, who live on authorized food, who have perceived the void, the Unconditioned, the Absolute, their way is difficult to understand, like the birds of the ether.

Forests are delightful; where the world finds no delight; there the passionless find delight, for they look not for pleasures.

Let a man overcome anger by love, evil by good, the greedy by liberality, the liar by truth.*

* How strikingly does the sentiment of this passage remind us of its analogy with the one expressed by the Nazarene, viz., "Overcome evil with good." Confucius enounces the same sentiment as the one

Some people are born again; evil-doers go to Hell; righteous people go to Heaven; those who are free from all worldly desires enter Nirvâna.*

All men tremble at punishment; all men fear death; remember that you are like unto them, and do not kill, nor cause slaughter.

taught in the "golden rule," although he expresses it negatively.

"The Christian system and the Buddhistic one, though differing from each other in their respective objects and ends as much as truth from error, have, it must be confessed, many striking features of an astonishing resemblance. There are many moral precepts equally commanded and in common by both creeds. It will not be considered rash to assert that most of the moral truths prescribed by the Gospel are to be met with in the Buddhistic Scriptures."— *Bishop Bigandet.*

*In Annotation 17 I have cited the views of several Sanskrit scholars on the meaning of Nirvana, who distinctly declare their disbelief that the phrase signifies annihilation. In confirmation of their views

He who for his own sake punishes or kills beings longing for life and happiness will not find happiness after death.

Do not speak harshly to any body; those who are spoken to will answer thee in the same way. Angry speech is painful; blows for blows will touch thee.

If like a trumpet trampled under foot, thou utter not, thou hast reached Nirvâna; anger is not known in thee.

As a cowherd with his staff gathers cows into the stable, so do Age and Death gather the life of man.

that the word denotes immortality, I add the following:

"The views indicated by 'Nirvana,' 'Dharma,' 'Karma,' and the other chief features of Buddhism, are at least the fruits of considerable study, and also of a firm conviction that a third of mankind would never have been brought to believe in blank abstractions or Nothingness as the issue and crown of Being."—*Edwin Arnold.*

Cut down the whole forest of lust, not the tree! When you have cut down every tree and every shrub, then, Bhikshus, you will be free!

So long as the love of man toward women, even the smallest, is not destroyed, so long is his mind in bondage, as the calf that drinks milk is to its mother.*

The fool does not know when he commits his evil deeds; but the wicked man burns by his own deeds, as if burnt by fire.

He who inflicts pain on innocent persons will soon come to one of these ten states: He will have cruel suffering, loss, injury of the body, heavy affliction, or loss of mind, or a misfortune

* The injunction given in this passage, to live down all affection for women, was undoubtedly designed by the Lord to apply to the ascetics, or the priesthood, and not to believers indiscriminately.

The celibacy of the Romish priesthood, and the same observed by the Shakers, the founders of these sectaries have rigidly prescribed.

of the king, or a fearful accusation, or loss of relatives, or destruction of treasures, or lightning-fire will burn his houses; and when his body is destroyed, the fool will go to Hell.

Not nakedness, not platted hair, not dirt, not fasting, or lying on the earth, not ribbing with dust, not sitting motionless, can purify a mortal who has not overcome desires.*

Is there a man in this world so restrained by humility that he does not mind reproof, as a well-trained horse the whip?

Like a well-trained horse when touched by the whip, be ye active and lively, and by faith, by virtue, by energy, by meditation, by discernment of the law, you will overcome this great pain (of reproof), perfect in knowledge, and in behavior, and never forgetful.

How is there laughter, how is there joy, as

*The rigid austerities of the Yoga system of asceticism the Lord Buddha did not commend to his followers.

this world is always burning? Why do you seek light, ye who are surrounded by darkness?

Look at this dressed-up lump, covered with wounds, joined together, sickly, full of many thoughts, which has no strength, no hold!

This body is wasted, full of sickness, and frail; this heap of corruption breaks to pieces, the life in it is death. Those white bones, like gourds thrown away in Autumn, what pleasure is there in looking at them!

After a frame has been made of the house, it is covered with flesh and blood, and there dwell in it old age and death, pride and deceit.

A man who has learnt little grows old like an ox; his flesh grows, but his knowledge does not grow.

Without ceasing, I shall run through a course of many births, looking for the maker of this tabernacle—and painful is birth again and again.

But now, maker of this tabernacle, hast thou been seen; thou shalt not make up this tabernacle again. All thy rafters are broken, thy ridge-pole is sundered, and I have attained to the extinction of all desires.*

Be not thoughtless! your thoughts draw yourself out of the evil, like an elephant sunk in mud.

If a man becomes fat and a great eater,

> *"Many a House of Life
> Hath held me—seeking ever him who wrought
> These prisons of the senses, sorrow-fraught;
> Sore was my ceaseless strife!
> But now,
> Thou builder of this tabernacle—Thou!
> I know Thee! Never shalt Thou build again
> These walls of pain,
> Nor raise the roof-tree of deceits, nor lay
> Fresh rafters on the clay;
> Broken thy house is, and the ridge-pole split!
> Delusion fashioned it!
> Safe pass I thence—deliverance to obtain."
>   *—Edwin Arnold.*

if he is sleepy and rolls himself about, that fool, like a hog fed on wash, is born again and again.

This mind of mine went formerly wandering about as it listed, as it pleased; but I shall now hold it thoroughly, as the rider who holds the hook holds in the furious elephant.

Self is the lord of self; who else could be the lord! With self well subdued, a man finds a lord such as few can find.

If an occasion arises, friends are pleasant; enjoyment is pleasant if it be mutual; a good work is pleasant in the hour of death; the giving up of all grief is pleasant.

The thirst of a thoughtless man grows like a creeper; he runs hither and thither, like a monkey seeking fruit in the forest.

If a man is tossed about by doubts, full of strong passions, and yearning only for what is delightful, his thirst will grow more and more, and he will indeed make his fetters strong.*

The fields are damaged by weeds; mankind, by passion; therefore a gift bestowed on the passionless brings great reward.

Without knowledge there is no meditation; without meditation there is no knowledge; he who has knowledge and meditation is near unto Nirvâna.

He who has traversed this mazy and impervious world and its vanity, who is through, and has reached the other shore, is thoughtful, guile-

---

*The following depiction of the play of the good and evil passions over man is both powerfully and artistically effected by the grandest poet Scotia ever bore:

"From Virtue's fount the purest joys out-well,
Sweet rills of thought that cheer the conscious soul;
While Vice pours forth its troubled streams of Hell,
The which, howe'er disguised, at last with dole
Will through the tortured breast their fiery torrent roll."
—*Thomson.*

less, free from doubts, free from attachment, and content, him I call indeed a Brahmana.

He who calls nothing his own, whether it be before, behind, or between, who is poor, and free from the love of the world, him I call indeed a Brahmana.

He who knows his former abodes, who sees Heaven and Hell, has reached the end of births, is perfect in knowledge, and a sage; he whose perfections are all perfect—him I call indeed a Brahmana.

The manly, the noble, the hero, the great sage, the conqueror, the guileless, the master, the Awakened, him indeed I call a Brahmana.*

* It is a noteworthy coincidence that while the writer was versifying the Life of Buddha, Mr. James Kinnersly Lewis, of London, England, was rendering in verse the *Dhammapada, or Path of Virtue.*

The following passage from the *Dhammapada*, which he versifies, exhibits his style of rhythmical numbers:

"Thy life has come to an end; thou art come

I will close these summarized citations from the teachings of the Great Teacher with the following beautiful parable from the works of Buddhagosha, who most touchingly depictures the Lord Buddha's interview with the bereaved Kisâgotimî:*

"This girl, who had lost an only child, went to Buddha, and, doing him homage, said: 'Lord and Master, do you know what medicine will cure my boy?' Buddha replied, 'I know some.' She asked, 'What medicine do you require?' He said, 'I want a handful of mustard-seed.' The girl promised to procure

near to Death (Yama), there is no resting-place for thee on the road, and thou hast no provision for thy journey."

"Thine earthly pilgrimage is now complete—
The road to Death hath now no resting-seat;
(Through Yama's waters deep thou soon wilt wade),
And for thy journey no provision made."

*I cite this parable from Max Müller's Lecture on "Buddhist Nihilism."

it for him; but Buddha continued: 'I require some mustard-seed taken from a house where no son, husband, parent, or slave, has died.' The girl said, 'Very good,' and went to ask for some at different houses. The people said, 'Here is some mustard-seed; take it.' Then she asked, 'In my friend's house has there died a son, a husband, a parent, or a slave?' They replied, 'Lady, what is this that you say? *The living are few, but the dead are many.*' Then she went to other houses; but one said, 'I have lost a son'; another, 'I have lost a daughter'; another, 'I have lost my parents'; another, 'I have lost my slave.'

"At last, not being able to find a single house where no one had died, from which to procure the mustard-seed, she began to think, 'This is a heavy task that I am engaged in. I am not the only one whose son is dead. In the whole Sâvathi country, everywhere, children are dying, parents are dying.' Thinking thus, she was seized with fear, and, putting away her affection for her child, she summoned up resolution, and left the dead body in a forest; then she went to Buddha, and paid him homage. He said to her, 'Have you procured the handful of mustard-seed?' 'I have not,' she replied; 'the people of the village told me, *The living are few, but the dead are many*.' Buddha said to her, 'You thought that you alone had lost a son; the law of death is that, among all living creatures, there is no permanence.'

"When Buddha had finished preaching the Law, Kisâgotimî was established in the reward of the novitiate; and all the assembly who heard the Law were established in the same reward.

"Some time afterward, when Kisâgotimî was one day engaged in the performance of her religious duties, she observed the lights (in the houses) now shining, now extinguished, and she began to reflect, 'My state is like these lamps.' Buddha, who was in the Gandhakuti building, sent his sacred appearance to her, just as if he himself was preaching, 'All living beings resemble the flame of these lamps, one moment lighted, the next extinguished; those only who have arrived at *Nirvâna* are at rest.'"

INVOCATION.

To thee, Lord Buddh', I voice this soul-felt prayer!
   Oh, hear thy servant plain 'neath sins bowed low!
The lowliest lot with thee he'd gladly share,
   In bowery spheres, dis'thralled from earth's dread woe!

Thy servant save, whene'er dire ills betide!
   No more henceforth he'll seek inglorious ease!
Thy matchless code he'll blaze both far and wide!
   Beyond the bourne of vasty realms and seas!

Yon stars may fall! fierce flames enwrap the world!
   A-dance in fiendish glee midst wild uproar!
Mount Meru's mighty mass to ruin hurled!
   Still o'er vast realms thou 'lt REIGN forevermore!

www.ingramcontent.com/pod-product-compliance
Lightning Source LLC
Chambersburg PA
CBHW020307170426
43202CB00008B/524